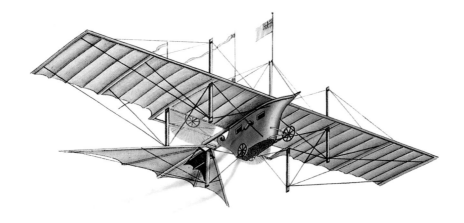

●Discovery
EDUCATION™

Published in 2014 by The Rosen Publishing Group, Inc.
29 East 21st Street, New York, NY 10010

Photo Credits: **KEY** tl=top left; tr=top right; cl=center left; cr=center right; bl=bottom left; br=bottom right; bg=background

CBT = Corbis; iS = istockphoto.com; LC = Library of Congress; N = NASA; SH = Shutterstock; TF = Topfoto; TPL = photolibrary.com

8-9bg iS; **9**tl CBT; **14**bg SH; **15**bg SH; tr TPL; **16**bg SH; **17**bg SH; tr TF; **18**bl iS; cl, cr LC; **19**br iS; br TF; **26**br iS; br, br, cr N; **26-27**bg iS; **32**bc SH

All illustrations copyright Weldon Owen Pty Ltd. **23**tl Peter Bull Art Studio

Weldon Owen Pty Ltd
Managing Director: Kay Scarlett
Creative Director: Sue Burk
Publisher: Helen Bateman
Senior Vice President, International Sales: Stuart Laurence
Vice President Sales North America: Ellen Towell
Administration Manager, International Sales: Kristine Ravn

Library of Congress Cataloging-in-Publication Data

Brasch, Nicolas.
 Conquering the sky / by Nicolas Brasch.
     pages cm. — (Discovery education : discoveries and inventions)
 Includes index.
 ISBN 978-1-4777-1331-0 (library binding) — ISBN 978-1-4777-1504-8 (pbk.) —
ISBN 978-1-4777-1505-5 (6-pack)
 1. Aeronautics—History—Juvenile literature. 2. Flight—History—Juvenile literature. I. Title.
 TL515.B6665 2014
 629.13—dc23
                                2012043613

Manufactured in the United States of America

CPSIA Compliance Information: Batch #S13PK3: For Further Information contact Rosen Publishing, New York, New York at 1-800-237-9932

DISCOVERIES AND INVENTIONS

CONQUERING THE SKY

NICOLAS BRASCH

Power

New Y

Contents

Flight In Nature

Flying is a vital survival skill for many creatures. They use flight to escape predators, or to observe and then attack prey. They also use flight to escape harsh weather conditions, such as storms and extreme cold. Flight is essential to their survival.

Ways of flying
The ways that different creatures fly have adapted according to the environment they live in.

Gliding, flapping, and hovering
Animals that fly use different motions to power through the air.

Birds
Hummingbirds are able to eat while hovering in the air.

Bat
The only mammals that can fly for lengthy periods are bats. They flap their wings.

Fish
Flying fish have fins that operate like wings. They glide through the air.

JUST BEAT IT!
Smaller insects beat their wings faster than larger insects. They also move more slowly through the air.

DRAGONFLY

SPEED PER HOUR: 15 miles (24 km)

WING BEATS PER SECOND: 35

INFO: A dragonfly beats its wings 8,400 times to travel 1 mile (1.6 km).

BUTTERFLY

SPEED PER HOUR: 14 miles (22.4 km)

WING BEATS PER SECOND: 10

INFO: A butterfly beats its wings 2,571 times to travel 1 mile (1.6 km).

Wind and air
Birds use wind and air in different ways when they fly.

Ocean winds
Albatross use strong ocean winds to soar through the air.

Hot air
Vultures use rising hot air to help them fly to great heights.

Updraft
Hawks catch winds that are forced upward over an obstacle.

Hovering dragonfly
A dragonfly has two sets of long wings that help it to hover.

Swallow in flight
A swallow has long wings and a forked tail that help it turn, bank, and swoop when hunting prey.

HONEYBEE

SPEED PER HOUR: 4 miles (6.4 km)

WING BEATS PER SECOND: 170

INFO: A honeybee beats its wings 117,000 times to travel 1 mile (1.6 km).

HOUSEFLY

SPEED PER HOUR: 9 miles (14.4 km)

WING BEATS PER SECOND: 170

INFO: A housefly beats its wings 68,034 times to travel 1 mile (1.6 km).

MOSQUITO

SPEED PER HOUR: 1 mile (1.6 km)

WING BEATS PER SECOND: 600

INFO: A mosquito beats its wings 2,160,000 times to travel 1 mile (1.6 km).

Myths and Legends

Flight has fascinated humans forever. It has been central to many stories and legends of different cultures through the ages. Human flight has also been a feature of art throughout history.

Isis
The Egyptian goddess Isis is often depicted with wings. This image comes from the myth that she turned herself into a hawk and hovered over the body of her dead husband, Osiris, fanning him back to life with her wings.

King Kai Kawus
In Persian legends, King Kai Kawus was carried on his golden throne by four eagles. The eagles were tempted by meat dangled in front of them. However, the eagles eventually got tired and the throne crashed to Earth.

Pegasus
The winged horse Pegasus appears in Greek mythology. Bellerophon, a Greek hero, captured Pegasus and rode him when he fought enemies and killed monsters.

Garuda

The creature Garuda appears in both Hindu and Buddhist mythology. It has a human body and the wings of a bird, often an eagle. In some legends, Garuda's enemy is Naga, a serpent with many heads.

Eilmer of Malmesbury

Around 1010, a monk named Eilmer of Malmesbury jumped from the tower of his abbey, flapping gigantic wings shaped like a bat's wings. But he forgot that flying creatures have tails to help them land, and he broke both his legs.

Icarus

Icarus, a character from Greek mythology, attempted to escape from King Minos's island. His father Daedalus made him wings from feathers joined together with wax, but Icarus flew too close to the Sun and the wax melted.

Scaring the enemy
Evidence of Chinese kites goes back more than 2,300 years. The colorful and often fearsome designs were used to signal during battle and to scare enemies.

Kites and Flying Machines

The earliest human attempts to fly were based on understanding the properties of wind, then designing craft that could be carried along on gusts of wind. Any mechanical parts were very basic and used only to change the craft's direction.

Box kite
Australian engineer Lawrence Hargrave invented the box kite. He once tested the strength of his kites by suspending himself in the air while hanging on to four box kites that were tied together.

From China to Japan
From China, kites spread to Japan about 1,300 years ago. The Japanese thought of the kites as religious symbols, flying to the heavens.

Wing designed to
flap like a bird's wing

Ahead of his time
Italian Leonardo da Vinci
(1452–1519) designed many
flying machines more than
400 years before real versions
were built and successfully
flown. This hang glider was
among his designs.

Harness device for
pilot to lie on

BATS AND BIRDS

Leonardo da Vinci took
inspiration for his early flying
machines from birds and bats.
These machines had flapping
wings, and were designed to
replicate the flight of birds and
bats as closely as possible.

Hand lever
Pulling the hand
lever made the
wings flap upward.

Foot pedal
Pressing the foot pedal
made the wings
flap downward.

Hot–air balloon
This balloon is kept flying by heating the air inside it using a controlled flame beneath its opening.

Hot-Air Balloons, Airships, and Gliders

The development of hot-air balloons was the result of scientific experiments and discoveries. But these can cause serious accidents and disasters, as well as triumphs. The mixing of gases with flames caused several mid-air explosions.

Parachute vent

Rip cord

Burners

Basket

Back to Earth
Balloon pilots land a craft by pulling a rip cord that opens the parachute vent and allows the hot air to escape.

EVOLUTION OF BALLOON FLIGHT

Throughout the 1800s, different gases and methods of power were tried to find the most effective way to fly through the air.

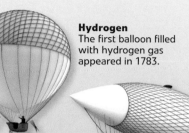

Hydrogen
The first balloon filled with hydrogen gas appeared in 1783.

Steam
A steam-powered balloon was flown in 1852.

Electricity
A balloon with an electric battery was flown in 1884.

Hindenburg disaster
The popularity of travel in large airships fell after the explosion of Hindenburg in New Jersey on May 6, 1937.

Gliding

Gliders are heavier-than-air craft that are not powered by an engine. They use air currents in the same way a bird does. In some gliders, the pilot is on the outside of the craft; in others, the pilot sits in a cockpit similar to that of an engine-powered aircraft.

Climbing
Pushing the control bar causes the glider to climb.

Diving
Pulling back on the control bar causes the glider to dive.

Turning
The glider turns when the pilot shifts his body to the side.

Éole
The propellers were turned by a steam engine.

Early Aircraft

Like most inventions throughout history, no one person can be credited as the inventor of the airplane. Certain inventions and scientific breakthroughs, such as the steam engine, led to further advances. And as with almost all areas of science, failures led to further experiments, tests, and trials that eventually brought success. Here are some of the earliest attempts to create heavier-than-air craft.

Model
William Henson's design was built only as a model.

1842
William Henson designed an airplane powered by a steam engine that turned two propellers.

1890
This batlike aircraft, Éole, was built by French engineer Clément Ader, and apparently flew about 160 feet (50 m) while a few inches (cm) above the ground.

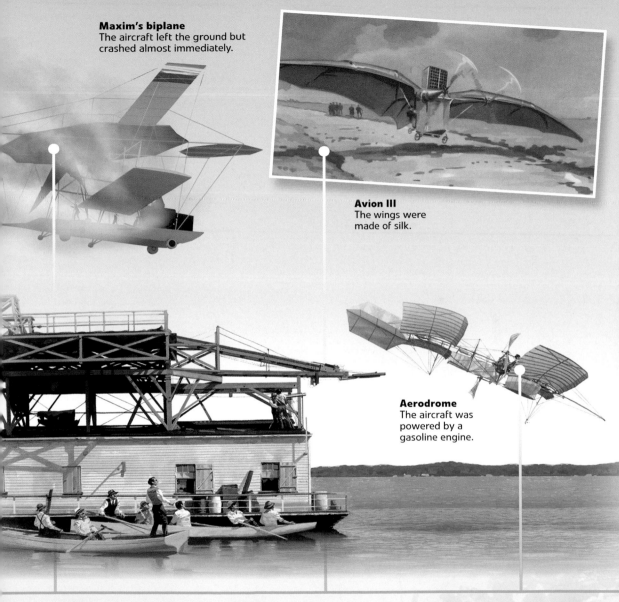

Maxim's biplane
The aircraft left the ground but crashed almost immediately.

Avion III
The wings were made of silk.

Aerodrome
The aircraft was powered by a gasoline engine.

1894
American inventor, Hiram Maxim built a biplane powered by two steam engines. He simply wanted a craft that could take off from the ground.

1897
Clément Ader claimed that he flew Avion III a distance of about 330 yards (300 m). However, there are doubts that such a flight took place.

1903
American Samuel Langley built the Aerodrome. The first flight ended with the plane plunging into the water just next to the platform.

Flyer
Orville and Wilbur Wright took turns flying their aircraft.

Airplane-car
This craft made several short hops in the air.

14-bis
The aircraft was built out of bamboo and canvas.

1903
The Wright brothers conducted the first successful flight of a heavier-than-air craft, at Kitty Hawk, North Carolina. Their craft took off from the ground and sustained flight for several seconds before landing.

1906
A Brazilian aviator, Alberto Santos-Dumont, based the design of his aircraft, the 14-bis, on the design of the box kite. He conducted the test flight in France in October 1906.

1906–1907
The Romanian inventor Trajan Vuia combined the features of a motorcar and an airplane to make his heavier-than-air craft. He added wings and a propeller to a four-wheeled vehicle.

Blériot
The Frenchman designed and built hundreds of aircraft.

Multiplane
Phillips flew his craft 500 feet (152 m).

1907
Englishman Horatio Phillips believed that an aircraft's wings were the key to successful flight—and the more wings, the greater the chances of success. His 1907 version had 200 wings.

1909
The French engineer Louis Blériot crossed the English Channel in his plane, Blériot XI. He flew without a compass or map from Calais, France, to Dover, England, in 37 minutes.

Famous Flights

Since the early 1900s, there have been a number of historic air flights. Some were over a distance of only a few hundred yards (m); others were across vast bodies of water. They were famous because they were firsts or because they played a major part in advancing the development of human flight.

The Wright brothers
Orville and Wilbur Wright owned a bicycle shop, and built and sold kites to finance their interest in designing and building aircraft. On December 17, 1903, Orville flew their plane a distance of 120 feet (37 m). Later that day, Wilbur flew the plane 850 feet (260 m).

Heads or tails?
Orville (left) and Wilbur flipped a coin to see who would fly their plane first.

Louis Blériot

On July 25, 1909, Frenchman Louis Blériot became the first person to fly across the English Channel. Strong winds and an overheated engine caused his plane to crash-land in Dover, England—but at least he had made it.

Igor Sikorsky

Russian aviator Igor Sikorsky designed and built the first four-engine plane. In 1914, he flew such a plane 800 miles (1,290 km) from St. Petersburg to Kiev, stopping only twice. By doing so, he proved that long-distance air travel was possible.

Spirit of St. Louis

In May 1927, American aviator Charles Lindbergh flew solo, nonstop from New York to Paris. This was the first such flight and it took 33 hours, 30 minutes.

Amelia Earhart

In 1932, American aviator Amelia Earhart became the first woman to fly solo, nonstop across the Atlantic Ocean. In 1937 she disappeared in the Pacific while attempting to fly around the world.

Propellers to Jets

For more than 30 years—from the time that the Wright brothers first took to the air—propeller power ruled the sky. The propellers were turned by an engine, creating thrust that, combined with lift, sent the aircraft into the air. But in 1939, the invention of the jet engine changed airplane design and mechanics forever.

Seaplanes
The development of the seaplane in the late 1930s enabled an American explorer, Richard Archbold, to investigate both the land and water in and around the Pacific island of New Guinea in 1938.

THE JET AGE

Jet engines work by burning air that enters the engine, thereby creating thrust that propels the airplane forward. The jet engine was developed in the 1930s by Frank Whittle and Hans von Ohain, although they did not work together on the idea.

First jet plane

On August 27, 1939, the Heinkel He 178 became the first aircraft to be powered by a jet engine. The air entered the plane through the nose and was directed to the engine.

Turbojet engine

Air enters the turbojet engine and is directed into the compression chamber where fuel is burned. When the air is heated, gases are expelled, creating thrust.

KEY
- Intake: cold air
- Combustion chamber: burning fuel and heated air
- Exit: hot exhaust gases

German ace

German fighter pilot Egon Koepsch scored nine air victories during World War I.

US dogfighter

The American SPAD XIII plane was involved in many dogfights during World War I.

Deadly dogfights

During World War I (1914–1918), propeller-powered planes held battles in the air. These were known as dogfights. The pilots drew the enemy planes as close as possible, then fired at them. At the same time, they performed moves to make sure they were not hit by the enemy.

Passenger Aircraft

The first airplanes carried only one or two passengers. But almost as soon as planes began appearing in the air, individuals and companies started thinking about the possibilities of flying large numbers of people over long distances. This would involve large aircraft that could fly for a long time without needing to stop. It seemed almost impossible in the early 1900s, but then so had the idea of airplanes themselves just a few years before.

1919
The Handley Page W8 seated 15 passengers and flew from London to Europe. In this plane, the pilot sat in an open cockpit.

1935
The Douglas DC-3 dramatically changed air travel. It could fly for longer and carry more passengers than other planes. A flight across the United States took the DC-3 only 17 hours.

1950
The De Havilland DH106 Comet was the world's first passenger jet airliner. After several accidents in the early 1950s this plane was redesigned. Later versions had a long life and commercial success.

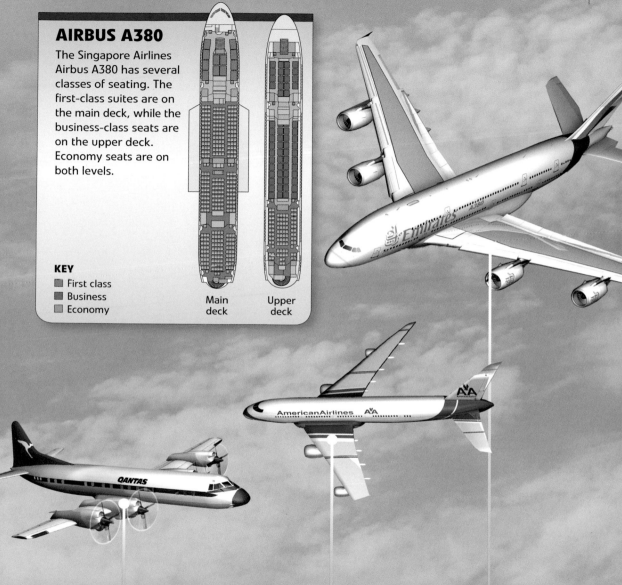

AIRBUS A380

The Singapore Airlines Airbus A380 has several classes of seating. The first-class suites are on the main deck, while the business-class seats are on the upper deck. Economy seats are on both levels.

KEY

- First class
- Business
- Economy

Main deck   Upper deck

1957

The Lockheed L-188 Electra was built for short to medium routes. It could carry 60–70 passengers. Initially popular as passenger planes, most of the aircraft are now used as freight carriers.

1970

The first so-called "jumbo jet," the Boeing 747, was capable of flying up to 524 passengers for long distances. One of its key features was its wide body.

2005

The Airbus A380 is a double-deck, wide-bodied plane that is capable of transporting up to 853 passengers long distances. It is sometimes referred to as the "superjumbo."

Stabilizer
The horizontal stabilizer could be adjusted to help control the aircraft.

Fuselage
The fuselage or body of the plane, was designed in the shape of a machine gun bullet.

6062

Plume
The powerful engine generated 6,000 pounds (2,722 kg) of thrust.

Wings
The thin wings were designed especially to withstand the pressure of supersonic flight.

Supersonic

S upersonic means flying faster than the speed of sound. This feat was first achieved by a piloted plane on October 14, 1947. The American pilot Chuck Yeager flew a Bell X-1 through the sound barrier. The speed of sound is known as Mach 1. The first pilot to fly Mach 2, twice the speed of sound, was Scott Crossfield in 1953.

Cockpit
The cockpit was tiny and the pilot had only limited visibility.

Probe
The narrow probe gathered information about air pressure during the flight.

Faster than sound

Glamorous Glennis was the name of the plane Chuck Yeager used to fly faster than the speed of sound. The plane was named for his wife.

PROVING THEM WRONG

At fast speeds, airplanes create pressure waves. When they approach Mach 1, the waves become shockwaves, which have enormous pressure. Before Chuck Yeager broke the sound barrier, many people believed that the existence of shockwaves made such a feat impossible.

Subsonic
Below Mach 1, pressure waves radiate both behind and in front of an airplane.

Transonic
At Mach 1 (transonic), the airplane catches up to the pressure waves, which then build up into a shockwave.

Supersonic
Above Mach 1, the shockwaves form a cone and erupt into a sonic boom when the cone hits the ground.

The speed record for piloted flight within Earth's atmosphere is Mach 6.72, set by William "Pete" Knight on October 3, 1967.

Into Space

Once humans had created aircraft to fly them around Earth, they set their minds on a bigger challenge—space. The main obstacle to sending humans into space was creating enough power to allow a craft to leave Earth's atmosphere without gravity forcing the craft back to the ground. The amount of fuel required would be so heavy and so potentially dangerous that many doubted such a mission was possible.

Saturn V
The most successful rocket was the Saturn V, which flew all the Apollo and Skylab missions from 1967 to 1973. Among these flights was Apollo 11, which landed the first humans on the Moon.

S-II second stage
The engine that boosted the third stage and the modules to a height of 114 miles (183 km)

S-IC first stage
The engine that boosted the upper parts of the craft to a height of 38 miles (61 km)

Escape tower
A rocket that could pull the Command Module from the rest of the craft

Command Module
Home to the astronauts during a flight

Lunar Module
The part of the craft that landed on the Moon

S-IVB third stage
The engine that propelled the craft away from Earth and toward the Moon

We have liftoff
Stage 1 burned for two and a half minutes. Stage 2 burned for six minutes. Stage 3 burned for about two and a half minutes.

S-IC LOX tank
Cold liquid oxygen that allowed liquid fuel to burn in space

S-IC fuel tank
Kerosene propelled the rocket from the ground.

SpaceShipOne

Until 2004, all flights into space were funded by governments. However, SpaceShipOne, which flew into space on June 21, 2004, was privately owned. It was not launched from the ground but air-launched from another aircraft, White Knight, from a height of 50,000 feet (15,240 m). The flight lasted about 30 minutes. Private companies are interested in space flight in the same way they saw the potential for long-distance passenger airplane flights almost 100 years ago. Passenger space flights may still seem like a dream, but so did passenger airplane flights then.

1 SpaceShipOne
Does not break into sections on re-entry. The entire craft returns to Earth.

2 SpaceShipTwo
Will fit two pilots and six passengers for a two-and-a-half-hour space flight.

3 Space station
Could be used for docking spacecraft and even as a hotel for space tourists.

Parade of Aircraft

FLYER (1903)

LENGTH: 21 ft. (6.4 m)

WINGSPAN: 40.4 ft. (12.3 m)

WEIGHT: 605 lb. (274 kg)

BLÉRIOT XI (1909)

LENGTH: 26 ft. (8 m)

WINGSPAN: 25.6 ft. (7.8 m)

WEIGHT: 507 lb. (230 kg)

IL'YA MUROMETS (1914)

LENGTH: 57.4 ft. (17.5 m)

WINGSPAN: 113 ft. (34.5 m)

WEIGHT: 6,930 lb. (3,150 kg)

HEINKEL HE 178 (1939)

LENGTH: 24.6 ft. (7.5 m)

WINGSPAN: 23.6 ft. (7.2 m)

WEIGHT: 3,572 lb. (1,620 kg)

DOUGLAS DC-3 (1935)

LENGTH: 64.6 ft. (19.7 m)

WINGSPAN: 95 ft. (29 m)

WEIGHT: 18,300 lb. (8,300 kg)

CONSOLIDATED PBY CATALINA (1935)

LENGTH: 64 ft. (19.5 m)

WINGSPAN: 104 ft. (31.7 m)

WEIGHT: 20,910 lb. (9,485 kg)

AVRO LANCASTER (1941)

LENGTH: 69.6 ft. (21.2 m)

WINGSPAN: 102 ft. (31.1 m)

WEIGHT: 36,828 lb. (16,705 kg)

BOEING 747 (1970)

LENGTH: 231.6 ft. (70.6 m)

WINGSPAN: 195.5 ft. (59.6 m)

WEIGHT: 358,000 lb. (162,400 kg)

F/A-18 HORNET (1978)

LENGTH: 55.8 ft. (17 m)

WINGSPAN: 37.4 ft. (11.4 m)

WEIGHT: 23,000 lb. (10,400 kg)

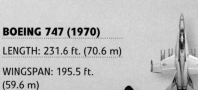

NIGHTHAWK F-117 (1981)

LENGTH: 65.9 ft. (20.1 m)

WINGSPAN: 43.3 ft. (13.2 m)

WEIGHT: 29,500 lb. (13,380 kg)

SPACE SHUTTLE ATLANTIS (1985)

LENGTH: 122.2 ft. (37.2 m)

WINGSPAN: 78.1 ft. (23.8 m)

WEIGHT: 172,000 lb. (78,000 kg)

W8 HANDLEY BIPLANE (1919)

LENGTH: 60 ft. (18.3 m)

WINGSPAN: 75 ft. (22.9 m)

WEIGHT: 8,600 lb. (3,910 kg)

WEDDELL–WILLIAMS (1932)

LENGTH: 23.3 ft. (7.1 m)

WINGSPAN: 26.6 ft. (8.1 m)

WEIGHT: 1,510 lb. (685 kg)

SPAD XIII (1917)

LENGTH: 20.7 ft. (6.3 m)

WINGSPAN: 26.9 ft. (8.2 m)

WEIGHT: 1,254 lb. (569 kg)

GEE BEE (1932)

LENGTH: 17.7 ft. (5.4 m)

WINGSPAN: 25 ft. (7.6 m)

WEIGHT: 1,840 lb. (834 kg)

FOKKER D.VII (1918)

LENGTH: 22.6 ft. (6.9 m)

WINGSPAN: 29 ft. (8.9 m)

WEIGHT: 1,540 lb. (698 kg)

DE HAVILLAND COMET (1950)

LENGTH: 112 ft. (34 m)

WINGSPAN: 115 ft. (35 m)

WEIGHT: 75,400 lb. (34,200 kg)

LOCKHEED L–188 ELECTRA (1957)

LENGTH: 104 ft. (31.8 m)

WINGSPAN: 99 ft. (30.2 m)

WEIGHT: 61,500 lb. (27,895 kg)

BELL X–1 (1947)

LENGTH: 30.8 ft. (9.4 m)

WINGSPAN: 28 ft. (8.5 m)

WEIGHT: 7,000 lb. (3,175 kg)

LEARJET 45 (1995)

LENGTH: 58 ft. (17.7 m)

WINGSPAN: 47.9 ft. (14.6 m)

WEIGHT: 13,695 lb. (6,212 kg)

A320 (1987)

LENGTH: 123 ft. (37.6 m)

WINGSPAN: 111.9 ft. (34.1 m)

WEIGHT: 93,079 lb. (42,220 kg)

F–22 RAPTOR (1997)

LENGTH: 62 ft. (18.9 m)

WINGSPAN: 44.6 ft. (13.6 m)

WEIGHT: 43,431 lb. (19,700 kg)

SPACESHIPONE (2004)

LENGTH: 28 ft. (8.5 m)

WINGSPAN: 27 ft. (8.2 m)

WEIGHT: 2,645 lb. (1,200 kg)

A380 (2005)

LENGTH: 239.5 ft. (73 m)

WINGSPAN: 262 ft. (79.8 m)

WEIGHT: 610,200 lb. (276,800 kg)

SPACESHIPTWO

LENGTH: 60 ft. (18.3 m)

WINGSPAN: 27 ft. (8.3 m)

WEIGHT: unknown

Mix and Match

Throughout this book, many of the aviation pioneers have been linked to particular aircraft. Here, they have all been mixed up. You have to match the aviation pioneer on the left with their plane on the right. The answers are at the bottom of the page.

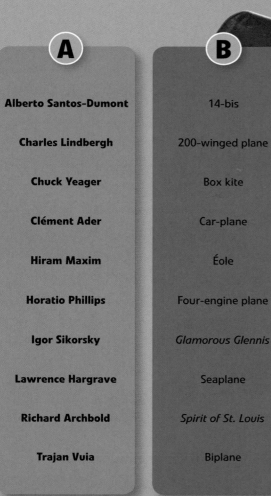

A	**B**
Alberto Santos–Dumont	14-bis
Charles Lindbergh	200–winged plane
Chuck Yeager	Box kite
Clément Ader	Car-plane
Hiram Maxim	Éole
Horatio Phillips	Four-engine plane
Igor Sikorsky	*Glamorous Glennis*
Lawrence Hargrave	Seaplane
Richard Archbold	*Spirit of St. Louis*
Trajan Vuia	Biplane

Answers: Alberto Santos-Dumont—14-bis; Charles Lindbergh—*Spirit of St. Louis*; Chuck Yeager—*Glamorous Glennis*; Clément Ader—Éole; Hiram Maxim—Biplane; Horatio Phillips—200-winged plane; Igor Sikorsky—Four-engine plane; Lawrence Hargrave—Box kite; Richard Archbold—Seaplane; Trajan Vuia—car-plane

Glossary

advancing (ud-VAN-sing)
Going forward.

aviator (AY-vee-ay-ter)
A pilot.

bank (BANK) To tilt.

chamber (CHAYM-bur)
An enclosed space.

cockpit (KOK-pit)
A space in an aircraft where
the pilot sits.

compass (KUM-pus)
An instrument that
indicates direction.

compression
(kum-PREH-shun) The act of
pushing things together.

depicted (dih-PIKT-ed)
Represented.

dogfight (DOG-fyt)
A battle in the air between
two war planes.

evolution
(eh-vuh-LOO-shun) A process
of change.

expelled (ek-SPELD)
Thrown out.

fuselage (FYOO-suh-loj)
The body of an airplane.

harness (HAR-nes)
An arrangement of straps
used to hold down a body.

kerosene
(kehr-uh-SEEN) A thin oil.

lever (LEH-vur) A handle
used to adjust a mechanism.

lift (LIFT) Upward force.

module (MAH-jool) A unit
of a spacecraft.

mythology
(mih-THAH-luh-jee)
A group of traditional
stories associated with a
particular culture.

Persia (PER-zhuh)
The former name of the
country Iran.

plume (PLOOM) The smoke
that is expelled from the
engine of an airplane.

predator (PREH-duh-ter)
A creature that lives by killing
and eating other creatures.

prey (PRAY) An animal that
is hunted and killed for food.

probe (PROHB) A device
that collects information.

propeller (pruh-PEL-er)
A device that pushes an
aircraft or boat forward.

rip cord (RIP KORD) A cord
pulled to release gas from
a balloon.

solo (SOH-loh)
On one's own.

sonic boom
(SAH-nik BOOM) A large
noise that occurs when a
plane flies faster than the
speed of sound.

stabilizer
(STAY-buh-ly-zer) A device
that keeps an airplane from
tipping over.

subsonic (sub-SAH-nik)
Slower than the speed
of sound.

supersonic
(soo-per-SAH-nik) Faster than
the speed of sound.

suspending
(suh-SPEND-ing) Hanging.

sustained (suh-STAYND)
Continued.

thrust (THRUST) Force.

turbine (TER-byn)
A machine that uses blades
or similar instruments to
convert the energy from, for
example, a liquid into
mechanical power.

vent (VENT) An opening
that provides an escape
for gases, steam, liquids,
or fumes.

Index

A

A320 29
A380 29
Ader, Clément 14, 15, 30
Aerodrome 15
Airbus A380 23
albatross 7
Apollo 11 26
Archbold, Richard 20, 30
Avro Lancaster 28

B

bats 6, 9, 11, 14
Bell X-1 24, 29
biplane 15, 29, 30
Boeing 747 23, 28
box kite 10, 16, 30
butterflies 6

C

car-plane 16, 30
Consolidated PBY Catalina 28
Crossfield, Scott 24

D

da Vinci, Leonardo 11
De Havilland DH106 Comet 22, 29

Douglas DC-3 22, 28
dragonflies 6, 7

E

Earhart, Amelia 19
English Channel 17, 19
Éole 14

F

F-22 Raptor 29
F/A-18 Hornet 28
Flyer 16, 28
flying fish 6
Fokker D.VIII 29
four-engine plane 19, 30
14-bis 16, 30

G

Garuda 9
Gee Bee 29
glider 13

H

hang glider 11
Hargrave, Lawrence 10, 30
Heinkel He 21, 28
Henson, William 14
Hindenburg 13
hot-air balloon 12, 13

I

Icarus 9
Il'Ya Muromets 28
Isis 8

J

jet engine 20, 21
jumbo jet 23

K

Kai Kawus, King 8
Koepsch, Egon 21

L

Langley, Samuel 15
Lindbergh, Charles 19, 30
Lockheed L-188 Electra 23, 29

M

Maxim, Hiram 15, 30
mosquitoes 7

N

Nighthawk F-117 28

P

Pegasus 8
Phillips, Horatio 17, 30

S

Santos-Dumont, Alberto 16, 30
Saturn V 26
seaplane 20, 30
Sikorsky, Igor 19, 30
SPAD XIII 21, 29
speed of sound 24, 25
Spirit of St. Louis 19, 30
supersonic 24, 25
swallows 7

U

updraft 7

V

von Ohain, Hans 21
Vuia, Trajan 16, 30

W

W8 Handley 29
Weddell-Williams 29
Wright, Orville 16, 18
Wright, Wilbur 16, 18

Y

Yeager, Chuck 24, 25, 30

Websites

Due to the changing nature of Internet links, PowerKids Press has developed an online list of websites related to the subject of this book. This site is updated regularly. Please use this link to access the list: www.powerkidslinks.com/disc/sky/